I WANT! I WANT!

T0161808

I WANT! I WANT!

Vicki Feaver

CAPE POETRY

1 3 5 7 9 10 8 6 4 2

Jonathan Cape, an imprint of Vintage,
20 Vauxhall Bridge Road,
London SW1V 2SA

Jonathan Cape is part of the Penguin Random House group of companies
whose addresses can be found at global.penguinrandomhouse.com

Penguin
Random House
UK

First published by Jonathan Cape in 2019

penguin.co.uk/vintage

A CIP catalogue record for this book is available
from the British Library

ISBN 9781787331815

Typeset in 11/13 pt Bembo by Jouve (UK), Milton Keynes
Printed and bound in Great Britain by TJ International Ltd, Padstow, Cornwall

Penguin Random House is committed to a sustainable future for
our business, our readers and our planet. This book is made
from Forest Stewardship Council® certified paper.

for my sister Génie
my grandchildren Esther, Holly, Eve, Enid,
Arthur, Oliver, Daniel and Agnes
my daughters Jane, Emily and Jessica
my son Silas who gave me my first poem
and in memory of my mother and father
and my uncle John (Jack) Fairhurst

My mother groand! my father wept.
Into the dangerous world I leapt:
Helpless, naked, piping loud;
Like a fiend hid in a cloud.

William Blake, 'Infant Sorrow'

I WANT! I WANT!

to William Blake

Stealing, aged eleven,
a cornflower-blue copy
of your poems, reading it
by torchlight, I decided
to be a poet: undaunted
as the child you pictured –
one foot on a ladder
reaching to the moon,
crying 'I want! I want!'

CONTENTS

THE LADDER

My family were perched
halfway up: my mother

pushing us from behind;
my father beginning to fail,

his legs shaking, hands
losing their grip.

When he plummeted
past me, I climbed on.

Primed with the mantra
Climb higher! Climb higher! –

running like a jingle
on a loop in my head –

I was expected to reach
the highest rungs.

★

I climbed for years,
the rungs rotting,

the top of the ladder
lost in fog, until,

my heart racing,
the air too thin to breathe,

I clung on in terror,
clenching my toes,

as if curled
like a monkey's

they could save me
from falling.

★

I longed for a parachute
to land me gently

on earth's springy turf,
restored to the child

who ran, fully-clothed,
into surf – bowled over

by waves that leapt up
like boisterous dogs;

who wandered alone,
through dark woods,

returning nettle-stung
and bramble-scratched;

who waded through black mud
to pick golden-globed flowers;

who wanted to discover
all the 'bright and beautiful' things

of the hymn she sang,
her voice soaring

into the rafters
of the school hall.

WAR BABY

In a house with gas masks
hanging in the hall

where the air was heavy
with waiting for news

of a soldier posted
'missing in action',

a mother and daughter
battled for possession

of the warm, milky bundle
of the daughter's baby.

Woken by the roar
of their explosions,

fear lodged in her body
like shrapnel. All her life

she was torn – her head
and her heart split in two:

as if, when words failed,
the women stumbled

from the rubble of their tirade
and, like battle-crazed soldiers,

hardly knowing
what they were doing,

each grabbed hold of an arm
and a plump little leg

and pulled.

VE DAY PHOTO

Toddler in a dress
of tiny blue flowers
and matching hat,
I stand on the front step
holding a Union Jack.

'Say "cheese"!' Daddy says,
wanting me to smile
for the camera.

But I grip my flag unsmiling,
solemn and proud
as if carrying the grief
of the whole house.

THE DOLL WITH A CHINA HEAD

When I was two-and-a-half
my mother disappeared
and came back with a baby
I tried to push off her lap.

So I wouldn't be jealous
she gave me the doll
her brother gave her
who was killed in the war;

showing me how to hold her
with one arm underneath
and one tight round
her slippery silk dress.

While my baby sister
guzzled milk, spurting
from my mother's breasts,
I nursed the doll – singing her

the song Grandma sang
as she rocked me,
pretending to drop me,
Rock-a-bye baby.

I don't remember the crash
as her head hit the floor,
only the narrow stairs
to the doll's hospital,

and my mother lifting me up
to the high counter,
and emptying a bag
of jagged pieces of scalp

and splinters of nose
and cheek and lips,
and the doll doctor saying,
'There's nothing we can do.'

THE LAWN-MOWER

At our old house,
a sickly rambler rose
struggled to find light
in a concrete back-yard.

I rode my tricycle
round and round
in a cramped circle
looking for a way out.

The new house had a garden
with a whole trellis of roses,
bordering a lawn
rioting with dandelions.

Daddy wheeled the lawn-mower
out of the garage,
pushing it up and down
in a pattern of bold stripes.

I walked beside him, watching
the cut grass shower
into the box, curious
to know how it worked.

'Don't!' he suddenly shouted,
as I poked my finger
towards the pale green haze
of the spinning blades.

THE SEWING-MACHINE

I could read its name – *SINGER* –
in a wreath of gold flowers
and smell the oil

squeezed into holes
like tiny mouths
in its shiny black shell.

Mummy was sewing
worn sheets, sides
to middle: guiding

the cloth with her fingers
frighteningly close
to the leaping needle.

When she pushed hard
on the pedal, there was a noise
like an engine revving

and the little silver foot
raced like a car
along the seams.

Daddy's coming!
Daddy's coming!
I chanted with my sister,

Daddy's coming!
Daddy's coming!
Daddy's coming!

faster and faster
as if his arrival
depended on it.

THE GIRL WHO LIKED
TO BE TICKLED

Lying on the slippery
rose-pink eiderdown
on my parents' bed,
giggling helplessly
as Daddy's long
pianist's fingers
trod delicately
as spider's legs
over the soles
of my bare feet;
shrieking as they raced
up my legs, climbing
the ladder of my ribs
and leapt into the crannies
under my arms and chin;
and, then, not knowing
where his fingers were
because they were scuttling
like mice all over my body,
I was screaming
for him to stop.

CROCUSES

When Grandma wasn't going to die
of pneumonia, and the doctor
told Mummy, 'Your nursing
has saved her life,'
she burst into tears.

I was smacked for picking
crocuses from the front lawn.
I dug holes in the grass
and tried to poke them back,
but Mummy said, 'It's too late for that.'

I carried the flowers upstairs
in a fold of my skirt,
heaping them on Grandma's bed –
blue and gold and purple –
like spilled jewels.

Grandma was coughing phlegm
into Jeyes toilet paper,
twisting each sheet
into a little parcel she posted
into a pot under her bed.

I passed her the thin,
disinfectant-smelling tissues,
worrying about wet-soil stains
seeping below the glowing petals
into her pale counterpane.

THE RABBIT HUTCH

No one wanted to share
a cramped dark space

with a boy who wheezed
and had patches of scaly,

oozing skin on his arms
and legs. So I climbed in,

nail-biter, stutterer,
who no one liked much either.

We crouched in silence
until the bell rang

for the end of break, filling
the creosote-smelling darkness

with the damp warmth
of our mingled breath.

THE WITCHES

My sister's screams
brought Mummy running:
Did you push her?
They drove to the hospital
leaving me alone in the house.

I read a book by the window
until I couldn't see the words.
Too scared to turn on the light,
I watched ghostly white roses
disappear into the dark.

Once, in a fever, I'd dreamed
of witches who lived in the loft
flying through the hatch.
Now they crouched
behind the wings of my chair.

I tried not to breathe,
pretending to be dead
like the stone girl in the churchyard,
or my sister, if all the blood
rolled out of her leg.

If she died, people
would think I was sad.
The witches knew the truth –
smelling my wickedness
with their long, hooked noses.

THE RECITAL

Pulled from sleep
to play for a neighbour
who my mother discovered
was a Professor of Music,
I stumbled through
a Mozart minuet.

'She's tired,' the professor said,
'she needs her sleep.'
'But has she got promise?'
my mother persisted.

BURNING BUSHES

My sister sowed pansies,
but I chose burning bushes
for the bush in the Bible, still blazing
when it should have been
a smouldering stump.

The pansies soon flowered,
little faces in glowing colours.
The burning bushes – flaming
in the picture on the packet –
remained puny and green.

I fed them with tea-leaves;
peed on them when no-one
was looking; as a last resort, prayed.
After a week of rain, they grew
as thick and feathery as firs.

In the heatwave that followed,
the tips turned pink, orange,
and, finally, a fiery-crimson spread
through every leaf and stem
like flames through a forest.

I dreamed of a tiger
stalking out to terrorise
my sister. 'Lie down!'
I'd order and it would lay
its striped head on my lap.

ELOCUTION

Lesson where we learned
to speak like the Queen:

'T-OW-N', we had to say
all round the class.

It was girls from council estates
who usually got picked on.

They pronounced town as 'tan' –
colour of sunburned skin.

We lived in Wollaton Park.
But my mother came from Wigan.

The way she said 'town'
meant a peaty pool in the hills.

The first time I got it wrong
the teacher told me to sit

with my hands on my head;
the next, with my arms in the air.

Finally, I was ordered to lie
on the splintery floor.

'Say "T-OW-N"!' she said again,
'pretend you're a princess.'

'Tarn,' I croaked, 'tarn',
in the voice of a little frog.

BOY WITH A KNIFE

He was standing in the middle
of the field, throwing a knife
from hand to hand: the boy

Mr Marshall brought down
at weekends, whispered
to be let out from borstal.

We heard thumps and squeals
coming from their caravan.
I was warned to keep away.

But I liked wounded things:
a baby rabbit the cat brought in;
birds with broken wings.

The boy aimed his knife
into a clump of lady's smock,
spearing a frog.

Dangling it by the leg,
he flung it into a gorse bush.
He looked down at my feet:

at sandals I'd woven from reeds
to resemble Roman sandals
in my history book,

at my bare toes, like a row
of tiny bald creatures
pleading for their lives.

PUGILIST

Uncle who was killed in the War;
whose boxing gloves, stitched
from padded orange leather,
were stored in the cupboard
above my bed; who haunted

our house, making my father
feel guilty for not fighting
and dying, and stopping
my mother and grandmother
from ever being happy.

On Remembrance Day,
when they sat in the gloom
behind closed curtains, watching
a tiny black-and-white telly
and weeping, as poppy wreaths

were laid on the cenotaph,
I sneaked out of the lounge
to dance on the lawn, paper poppy
pinned in my hair, leaping
and twirling in frosty grass.

That night, Uncle Jack
appeared in my bedroom,
jigging from foot to foot,
and throwing punches at me
with bunched orange fists.

I woke with a nosebleed:
a flow of scarlet drops
soaking my pillow and sheets
and an old towel, half-filling
the blue kitchen bowl.

THE TUNNEL

Wanting us out of the way
while they pored over brochures
of life in Rhodesia with servants
and swimming pools, our parents
sent us out for a walk.

No trains on Sundays, the boy said,
we can go through the tunnel.
I'd promised to look after my sister.
But I thought he might hold
my hand in the darkness.

We were treading over cinders
and sleepers deep under the hill,
when I heard a rumble like far-off thunder
and, looking back, saw the bright hole
of the entrance go black.

I thought of lying between the rails,
or squeezing against the tunnel wall.
But I was wearing my best, lime-green
shantung dress and, if it got dirty,
my mother would be furious.

So I grabbed my sister's hand
and we ran. And the angel
who sometimes intervenes
to save the lives of children
slowed the wheels of the train.

And we emerged, breathless
and blinking, into bright sun
in the cutting, just in time
before we were swallowed
by a cloud of smoke and steam.

GRANDMA'S BED

I unfold one of the old curtains,
tracing its washed-out pattern
of blue daffodils, pushing
my fingers through the holes
of cigarette burns.

And I remember the day
it was decided that Grandma
couldn't live any longer
in a house with my mother
without one killing the other.

My father fetched a mallet
to knock apart the stiff joints
of her bed. He strapped it
to the roof-rack, and drove us
from our road, where all the houses

had gardens, to a treeless street
in town where terraces rose
straight from the pavement.
We climbed dark stairs
to a cramped bedsit: grey nets,

a stained, beer-reeking carpet
and a geyser above the sink
that, when he turned on the gas
and held a lighted match to it,
exploded with a blue flash.

He was squatting on the floor
with his screwdriver kit –
my mother and grandmother
and me and my sister
standing behind him,

and the bed's strung-wire base
and brass rods and knobs
and lily-leaf flourishes
almost fitted together,
when I started to cry.

Then we were all crying,
like when there's a truce in a war,
and my father took the bed
to pieces again and strapped it
back on the car roof-rack.

The summer I walked round Venice
in bright yellow hot-pants
and a black strapless top,
and my mother said, *I wish
I'd never brought you.*

On the boat to Murano
I sat on the top deck alone,
shivering and burning
in the wind off the lagoon,
torn between jumping in,

or living for a dream
of a life beyond school
and exams and holidays
with my mother, imagined
from novels and films.

In the factory on the shore,
we watched men, bare
to the waist, muscled
like statues of the gods,
plunge globs of coloured glass

into white-hot furnaces:
their skill, before it cooled,
to blow glowing vases
and bowls; or to tease
the softened glass

into long thin strings
they drew through the air
in the shape of fish
and birds and animals.
I bought a tiny white cat,

so fragile and brittle
it broke on the way home.
My mother chose a gold-
flecked ruby ashtray
like a jellied heart.

THE DOVE

The day I walked with my mother
along the valley of the Dove –

crossing stepping stones, too risky
when the river was in spate,

climbing a crag and looking down
on its silver coils from above.

It was the closest we'd come,
as if the bird that carried

an olive twig in its beak
over the swirling waters

of the flood had circled us,
until, brushing picnic crumbs

from her lap, my mother stood up,
stepped closer to the sheer drop,

and said *I can feel something
pulling me towards the edge.*

BECAUSE SNOW HAD FALLEN

You wouldn't, would you?
my mother said, as we stood
facing each other, gripping tight
to the corners of a white sheet
and tugging it straight.

The word *sex* was never said.
But knowing what she meant
and not wanting to quarrel
on the night before I left home,
I promised *No* thinking *Yes.*

Next morning, as my father
drove me to the station,
I watched the back of his neck
turn scarlet, as he said,
You know where to kick?

In the end I lost my virginity
because snow had fallen
and, breathing the icy air,
I felt like Lara in *Dr Zhivago;*
and because the American scholar

who pulled me scarily fast
on a sledge, and taught me
to play strip-poker, poured me
tumblerfuls of bourbon
and wrote me a poem.

1974

The year Anne Sexton
sat in her red Cougar
with a glass of vodka
behind the closed doors
of her garage and drifted off
to its purring lullaby
in her mother's fur coat.

The year I read Emily Dickinson:
'This is the Hour of Lead –
Remembered, if outlived,
As Freezing persons, recollect the Snow –
First – Chill – then Stupor – then, the letting go –'

'What do you do?'
a man asked me at a party.
'What do you do in the afternoons?'

I was thirty-one:
the same age as Plath
when she turned on the gas.

'I'm a poet!' I lied
jolting myself to life:
a woman buried under ice
with words burning inside.

BRAMBLE ARM

In a dream, my right arm —
the arm that wields

my writing hand —
is encircled by brambles,

coiled from elbow to wrist
like barbed wire.

It could be a punishment
for unlocking the voice

I was taught as a child
to soften or silence.

Or a sign of its power —
a weak woman's arm

transformed into
a fearsome weapon.

Later in the dream, the arm
is swathed in bandages,

as if to hide or smother
the barbed stems.

But the gauze is stained
with blood and blackberry juice.

Under the wrapping
the bramble still lives:

roots twined round
sinew and bone;

spiked shoots
piercing the flesh.

HEDGEHOG GIRL

I was born bristling
with prickles. My mother
shaved me with a razor.

When the prickles grew back –
longer, thicker, sharper –
she pulled them out with tweezers.

When they sprouted again –
a pelt of spiky armour –
she chased after me with pliers.

I ran away and hid in the woods.
Sniffed out by snarling dogs,
I rolled into a ball.

I forgot I was a girl
until a forester arrived
to fell a towering pine.

I watched in a swoon
as he swung his axe –
driving the blade

deeper and deeper
into the bright wood.
The tree shrieked, swayed,

and fell with a crash.
The forester turned,
flicked a lock of glossy

black hair from his eyes
and stared through me
as if I was air.

I ran to the pool's mirror:
saw a girl as spiky
as gorse on the moor.

I built a fire with dry branches.
Rolling first in claggy clay
I ran through the flames.

Three times, I ran through fire
to become the woman
of a man's desire.

Three times, I tried and failed
to tame my fierce nature.
And now I live alone:

my spines re-grown,
a spiky thicket
around my heart.

SNOW QUEEN

I'd melt in your houses.
I hide in blue shadows,
appearing only at night:

a bride in a glittering veil,
pale and shining
as if lit from inside.

You offer me a snowman:
a frozen dummy
with eyes of coal.

But I want a husband
with a heart in my bed,
who'll lie with me

where the snow's blown
layer on layer like petals,
drifting to sleep in a heat

like hot sand, like ashes,
the water in his blood
turning to crystals of ice.

MERMAID

Sick of combing tangles
from my salt-sticky hair,
of my voice being lost
in the sea's hiss and roar,
I decided, one stormy night,

to ride a wave to the shore,
urging it on like a horse
over sand and marram,
leaping hedges and walls,
before bolting out of control.

Bursting through the door
of a great granite church,
it left me marooned,
high and dry in a niche
on the roof of a tomb –

muscular fish-tail
immovably wedged,
stone curls impeccably neat
and sweet siren songs
locked in my throat.

PEASANT DOLL

Painted on, my red dress,
patterned with tiny white flowers,
will never crumple; my scarf
never come undone.

My features are painted, too.
I can't open my mouth
to scream, or yawn,
or offer an opinion.

The expression on my face
permanently sweet
and serene, it seems
that I share nothing

with flesh-and-blood women.
Except, under the hollow
of my plastic skirt,
I'm balanced on a spike.

THE GOD OF SUGAR

(Sugar Shed, Greenock)

Cavernous and empty now –
no shouts of dockers,
no barefoot women shovelling
molasses – it has the chill
and hush of a cathedral.

Like a pilgrim arrived at a shrine,
wanting something to touch
for a vision or a sign
that a saint or god is here,
I rub the tip of my finger

against the rough bricks
of the wall and lick: tasting
sweet dirt, seeing, shining
in the gloom, an obese boy –
like Elvis in a sequin suit.

What prayers should I offer
to this god of sugar?
It's too late for the child
who spooned golden syrup
from the green lion tin

to dribble amber pools
in her porridge; who stole
from her mother's purse
to buy red-tipped sugar cigarettes,
so I pray for the woman

who still craves sweetness:
savouring strawberries dipped
in the sugar dish, gobbets
of crystalised ginger, figs
almost rotten with ripeness.

THE SMELL OF RUBBER

Smell I half-hate
but am irresistibly
drawn to – of babies' teats
and the johnnies we used
in the attic of the vicarage;
a smell even more strongly
in my nostrils now
as I pour scalding water
into the floppy open mouth
of a hot water bottle:
hearing the burps
of squeezed-out
air-bubbles: something
about the longing to hold
and be held making me hug
the small, hot, pliable body
to my chest as I fall asleep,
though I know I'll wake
with it cold in my bed,
and stinging burn marks
branded on my skin
like fierce red kisses.

THE SCENT OF TOMATOES

Scent breathed in the steamy greenhouse –
my mother's nursery of brilliant babies
who repaid her nurture in a single season,

their vermilion ripeness an antidote
to blackness. It was her yearly ritual:
watering, feeding, and before the plants

had a chance to grow unruly, nipping out
unwanted shoots and binding the stems
to bamboo stakes. The first few tomatoes

to turn pale orange, she sliced triumphantly
into sandwiches. As they swelled and ripened,
she fed us tomatoes until we were sick of them

and they hung on the stems, skins split open,
oozing silvery seeds. The green and yellow ones
the sun had failed to ripen, she boiled

with vinegar to fill jars with chutney;
reserving a few to lay on the top shelf
of the airing cupboard where their scent,

clinging to sheets and towels, lingered –
leafy, lemony, and with a faint whiff
of urine like an animal's lair.

HEAD WARS

My mother and grandmother
live in my head, sparring
and throwing crockery

as they did fifty years ago
in their shared kitchen.
It's not just my mind

that's being wrecked.
A nerve carrying signals
to a vocal cord has died,

leaving it paralysed.
The nerve endings
in my feet are fraying.

I can still speak –
but my voice is fainter.
I can walk – but my toes burn

with the hot-ache I remember
from playing in the snow
and coming in to warm

freezing toes and fingers
by the fire. Pain numbed
by little blue pills, I can sleep.

But it's like sleeping
in a pram being pushed
along the edge of a precipice

by two acrimonious ghosts
squabbling over
who holds the handle.

BLUEPRINT FOR A MOTHER

I know how I want her:
smelling of plums and sweat
like my pen-friend's mother

and brave and clever
like those Old Testament heroines,
Judith and Deborah,

women not afraid to speak
their minds and, when
the cause was just, to fight.

She has to be strong enough
to kick the miserable, carping,
never-satisfied mother

out of my head; and patient
and resourceful enough
to live there instead:

a mother who'll help pass
the long night hours
telling stories and singing songs,

who'll put her arms round the girl,
young woman, older woman,
and even the grandmother –

all in there, huddled
in the dark, like a family
in a bomb shelter, frightened

of being blown apart.

THE WOMAN WHO MARRIED A MAN
WHO LOVED SILENCE

Tired of men who filled her head
with their words and left no room
for her own thoughts, she married
a man who loved silence.
He'd thought of becoming a monk.

They moved far away to a house
marooned among woods and fields.
Conversation was replaced
by the mewing of buzzards,
the eerily human coughs of sheep.

Eating, going for walks, making love,
happened silently, until, in the absence
of the little words and noises
that accompany the joining of bodies,
even talking by touch ceased.

She made plans to leave.
But stayed, year after year,
winter after winter, as rooted
in the place as the snowdrops,
buried in papery sleeves.

DEATH AND THE MAIDEN

He was there at her birth –
watching as she was delivered,
doll-size, six weeks early,
to a mother with perilously
high blood-pressure.

He stayed for her first cry;
then left, no longer interested
until her appendix threatened
to burst on a caravan holiday
in Wales. She was eleven:

next to her on the ward,
a woman who confided,
'Half my stomach's missing.'
One night, the curtains
closed round the woman's bed.

Next morning, it was empty.
He'd gone too, refusing
to return, even when
she called him, crying bitterly.
Though when she swallowed

a whole bottle of pills
he arrived to say, *Silly girl!*
He raced to the lonely lake
where a man took off his tie
and threatened to strangle her

and, when she opened her mouth
to scream and no sound
came out, he pinned

the man to the ground
while she ran into the trees.

When she swam too far out
into cold Cornish sea
and, too tired to struggle
against the current,
let her mouth and nose slip

under the water, he cupped
her chin in his hand
as a father might a child's,
lifting it above the waves
until she reached the beach.

And when she rode pillion
on a motorbike, doing a ton
on the switchback road
that runs along the Roman Wall
not caring if she held on

or let go, she felt his arms
round her waist, holding her safe.
After that, she didn't think
of Death for years.
And he had no reason

to think of her. But now,
though she can't see or hear him,
she senses that he's back:
creeping behind her
in velvet slippers.

THE SURGEON'S WIDOW

She dug all night in the company
of moths – drawn from the dark
to the bright beam of her torch –
recovering first his skull, last,
the phalanges of his toes.
Finally, at dawn, her bag full,
she carried her husband home.

She laid his bones, damp and cold
from the grave, on a rug
by the fire; then found a drill,
pliers, and a coil of wire.
Aided by the diagrams
in his anatomy books,
she reassembled his gaunt frame.

The night of their wedding,
he'd swung her off her feet,
waltzing her from room to room
before carrying her up to bed.
Now, she held him and danced
the same route, stumbling,
almost falling on the stairs.

Once, they'd made love in the bath.
Now, lifting him gently
into the tub, she washed him
like a muddy child,
scrubbing with a nailbrush
at green and amber stains
on his porous bones.

His hands she left till last –
soaping fingers famous
for their delicate skill
with her fingers, crooked
and clumsy with arthritis.
Finally, rinsing off grey suds,
she dried him with a warm towel.

She slept, as before his death,
his knees slotted into the crook
of her knees, her buttocks
cradled by his pelvis,
her head on the pillow
beside his, dreaming
of his breath on her neck.

THE BLUE WAVE

Do it now, say it now, don't be afraid.
Wilhelmina Barns-Graham

In my head there's a painting
done in your nineties
when just to lift your arm

was an effort: a single brave
upwards sweep with a wide
distemper brush, so loaded

with paint the canvas filled
with the glistening blue wall
of a wave before it falls.

FORGETFULNESS

When my memory
was a film library
with a keen curator

who knew precisely
where to find clips
of every word

I wished unsaid,
or deed undone,
to play back to me

on sleepless nights,
I'd have welcomed her
muddling the reels.

But now the curator's
retired, the ordered
shelves are in chaos.

I roam the racks
without a guide
searching for scenes

I've lost. Sometimes,
not able to remember
what I'm searching for,

I find Forgetfulness
kneeling on the floor –
an old woman, pale

and worried as a ghost,
rummaging in a tangle
of shiny black ribbons.

THE LARDER

Yesterday it was the blaze
of a broom bush; the day before

the peppermint whiff
of a beeswax lip-balm.

Each day, I fill the shelves
with things to remember.

Today, it's the powdery bloom
on the skin of a blueberry,

turning it, cold from the fridge,
between my thumb and finger;

noticing the petal-shaped crater
where the flower withered

and the small hole
where it was pulled

from the stalk; crushing
its tangy pulp on my tongue.

POMEGRANATE JUICE

Head propped on pillows,
my face, in the mirror,
spectral with the pallor
winter lends old skin,

I gaze out over
the shining ridges
of my duvet's ice-field
to snow-bound hills

where my soul will fly
when she decides
it's time to leave
my failing body.

My mouth as dry
as if I'd eaten
a bowl of ashes,
I remember the beaker

of pomegranate juice
I bought from a stall
in the baking streets
of Erbil – freshly squeezed

from a revolving drum
of crimson seeds –
the gleaming juice
in the silver loving cup

Hades shared
with Persephone
to toast her arrival
in the Underworld.

THE CHERRY TREE

When the cold, colourless months
of winter stretched endlessly,
I waited for the flowering
of the cherry tree
like a child counting
the days to a birthday.

Growing older, the months
speeded up: the blossom,
opening in March, scorched
by frost, or quickly blown
from the branches to lie
rain-sodden on the lawn.

If the tree hadn't towered
so huge and unwieldy,
I'd have erected a tent
to hold back the buds.
But while I shrank,
it rose even higher.

I was sure the tree
would outlive me:
sap rising up the trunk
long after I was ash.
But now, strangled by ivy,
it's weakening, too.

Only this moment is certain,
both of us here and alive:
a cherry tree flowering;
a woman gazing at branches
clotted with pink blossom
and searching for words.

THE BLACK BERET

Cashmere, the only wool
not to make my scalp itch,
it shields my ears from icy winds.

Yet it keeps getting lost –
dropped on lonely paths,
left behind in buses,

as if there's a woman
in my head who, seeing it,
again returned to me,

perched above
my pale face
in the mirror,

hears the tap-tap
of Blind Pew's stick,
dying away in the distance.

PRAYER AT SEVENTY

God of thresholds, guide
of souls between worlds,
have mercy on me:

God who, when I asked you
if I could pass my last years
with less anxiety,

changed me into a tiny spider
launching into the unknown
on a thread of gossamer;

and when I begged you
to let me be a bigger
fiercer creature,

made me a polar bear
leaping between
melting ice floes.

ASCENSION

As a child, I wanted to live
in a room at the top of a tower
with a lockable trapdoor.

I've ended up in a bungalow,
in a valley hemmed in by hills,
often cut off by snow,

but under the flightpath
of wintering pinkfoots,
honking overhead

in a language as unintelligible
as the wavering script
they scrawl across the sky.

When the geese leave,
heading for Greenland in spring,
I watch buzzards riding

the thermals, or attacked
by angry crows, flocks of gulls
driven inland by gales.

On still days, hearing the roar
of a gas flame, I look up
to see hot-air balloons,

striped turquoise and lemon,
rising above the pines.
I'm too frightened

to go up in a basket.
But in my dreams I soar –
lifting into the air, without wings,

or even flapping my arms.
If only I could do it awake!
Trapped by snow,

vexing visitors,
or infirmity, I'd escape
through an open window.

SECOND CHILDHOOD

Some return, having lost
every memory in between,
to the only place they feel at home.

But even those who bolt
the door on childhood
return to its scenes in sleep.

I dreamed of my ashes
swilling with plankton
in the ocean's currents,

washed up on a beach
where my grandmother
dozed in a deckchair,

dressed for the cold wind
in a black straw hat
and thick winter coat.

I crouched beside her,
wearing only a sun-suit:
a child with long plaits

and a pale pinched face
digging her frozen toes
into the grains of sand.

TRAVELLING

One Christmas, I drank Buck's Fizz
on the top deck of a cruise ship
in the middle of the Indian Ocean

with three women in their late eighties –
one with a metal hip, two minus breasts –
all, like Tennyson's restless Ulysses,

buoyed by the belief that by living
permanently at sea they could go on
circling the world's oceans, and sitting

at the captain's table for ever.

BONE-HOUSE

I've always loved old houses
for the histories they hold.

Old bodies are the same.
My bowed head and neck

are evidence of hours
spent battling with words.

My belly-skin, stretched
by four babies, resembles

rippled sand on a beach
when the tide retreats.

My face's fretted lines
betray a lifetime as a worrier.

Foolish, when I think how safe
my life compared to poets

who linked 'bone' with 'house'
to forge a more accurate word

than 'body' for what living
was home to blood vessels

and vital organs, so vulnerable
to thrusts of spear and sword,

and dead, the spirit flown,
a corpse left lying on a battlefield,

revealed the bones it housed,
picked clean by circling crows.

THE HIDDEN LUNGS

Watching horses snorting
cloud towers into frosty air,
and, seeing my breath also,
normally unseen, pouring
from my open mouth,

I think of my hidden lungs,
swelling and shrinking
under the rise and fall
of my chest like coral-pink
under-sea sponges.

From the moment I plunged
from the womb's liquid dark
into dry bright air, and took
my first breath, my lungs
have never faltered.

I saw them once on an X-ray:
two dark shapes in a circle
of the ribs' standing stones.
With the viral pneumonia
that stilled the lungs

of my ninety-year-old mother,
the air-sacs, filled with fluid,
appear as white spots.
Her lungs laboured for days
seeming to shut down,

noisily starting up again.
I pictured her driving them on
like a pair of failing horses
harnessed to a chariot
pursued by wolves.

ALL KINDS OF HORSES

Usually, as a mind ages
it narrows: worst case
shrinks to a dark yard
where a broken nag stands,
blinkered and shackled.

But it's not impossible
for a curious mind
to go on expanding:
from paddock to pasture
to unfenced prairie

where all kinds of horses –
from retired hacks
to nervy thoroughbreds,
tough moorland ponies
and giant Clydesdales –

roam freely, rolling
in lush grass and clover,
and chomping prickly gorse
and wild rose bushes
that tickle their jaws.

HOME IS HERE, NOW

after Philip Larkin

Home is here now
at this table with its gouged
and scratched wood

where I'm peeling
an orange – the spray
from the zest sending

shivers up my nose,
and the bright rind
falling in a long curl.

It's the quiet time
at the end of the day:
no bird song, no wind;

just my in-and-out breaths
and the faint tearing of pith
parting from flesh.

CLEMENTINES

Past their best
when the thin peel
could be stripped off

in a single piece,
exposing fruits bursting
with sweet juice,

they're dried up, shrinking.
But I'm of an age
to want to honour

their decaying –
the grooves between
the segments

deepening;
their glowing colour
dulling and darkening;

to bear witness
as they collapse in
on themselves –

spent suns, casting
umber shadows
in the white dish.

THESE ROSES YOU GAVE ME

perfumed the kitchen
all through Christmas
and into the New Year.

Surviving the steamy wafts
of roasting meat,
they opened petals

the deep ruby velvet
of old theatre curtains
to reveal a maze

of shadowy crevasses.
Petals curling back now
and blackening at the edges,

the show's still not over.
Like elderly actresses,
performing until they drop,

one boasts an errant streak
of canary yellow, another,
a bush of gold stamens.

THE MOWER

When I was young and miserable,
a misfit and a rebel,
almost never out of trouble,
desperate to escape school,
time dawdled.
             Now I'm older
and happier and want it to go slower,
it's an out-of-control mower
careering through the borders
decapitating all the flowers.

BLACKBIRD SHOWER

I watch a blackbird
showering in a puddle,
yellow beak dancing
in the muddy water
like a chip of sun.

Swapping my wrinkled skin
and shrivelled spirit
for his glossy plumage
and *joie de vivre*,
I surprise myself

by airily lifting off
the floor, flying through
the window, and hopping
across the gravel
to a rain-filled pothole

where not even the danger
of the sparrowhawk patrolling
can spoil the pleasure
of sinking my breast
into its coolness,

then fluffing out my feathers
and shaking myself,
sending a spray
of glittering drops
over my back and wings.

MY BED

What in a fire I'd most want to save:
not, like Anne Bradstreet, watching

my household goods in flames
and attributing all to God,

but entering the smoke
before I can be stopped.

The house would burn like a marriage
leaving black grease and ash.

My bed I'd bring out intact:
brass coils jingling, zig-zag quilt,

stitched from poppy-red and cream
flower-printed cloth, frayed with use.

Bed where I embrace aloneness
whose limbs are any shape I want;

where I make in the only way I know,
again and again, in the envelope

of white soap-scented sheets,
a new world; where, in a corridor

between me and the sun, I see,
lit up in the firmament of dust,

the debris of my skin and hair
rising and falling in the air.

SHEDDING

Time to begin shedding:
to jettison the weight
of belongings

accumulated
and clung to
as if without them

I'd be as vulnerable
as a tortoise
stripped of its shell.

Time – before I'm thrown out
of the world with nothing,
a fretful ghost

rattling doors
and windows
to be let back in –

to become as light
as a moth flitting
through the night garden.

OLD WOMAN IN A FORSYTHIA BUSH

Bright bush of yellow stars
reaching out to me
with long bowed wands
among fields ringing
with blackbird songs

where lambs, licked into life
by sheep's rough tongues,
leap impossibly high
as if hung on strings
of a great puppeteer

who also dangled me
when young, inciting me
to strip off top and bra
to celebrate spring;
and, now I'm old,

whose arms have steered me
through the long dark corridors
of another winter, to sit
on this sunny seat, among
starry stems of forsythia,

buoyant again, as if sprung
from my body and floating
above it, like a seed flung
from the grey head
of a dandelion.

YOU ARE NOT

for my mother

You are not in these tulips,
not in their flailing stems
or shrivelled yellow petals
that alive you'd have painted;
not in the pearly wintry sky
or the scarred slopes of the hill
that before your legs failed
you'd have climbed;
not in the spiky firs
or eddies and swirls of the river,
or in its still sandy pools
where in your youth
you'd have swum;
not in the first drizzle of snow,
or in the deer that hangs
in the larder with black hooves
and long delicate legs,
not in its heart or liver
that we ate last night for supper
and you would have relished.

You are not anywhere
who loved all the things I love
but I couldn't talk to;
who still loom in my head
like a giantess.
       Yet I remember
hauling you out of the bath,
tugging on arms I was afraid
of pulling from their sockets;
then drying you and helping you

to dress, before guiding you
down slippery stone steps
to watch flycatcher chicks
leaving the nest, hearing
the *peep peep peep*
of their mother's warning call.

FINDING MY FATHER

(to the tune of the Old Hundred)

Hearing the slow tune of a hymn
I step into my childhood world
and find you in an organ loft
coaxing the keys to solemn chords.

I sit beside you on the stool
so close I smell your sour breath.
Your long thin feet jab out the bass.
You whistle softly through your teeth.

You hold me in a rubber ring
in shallow sea at Kessingland:
a man who never learnt to swim,
without your specs are almost blind.

Your black wool swimsuit's like a girl's;
your freckled skin's burned candy pink.
I dig until I've buried you
in cold damp sand up to your neck.

You spit the sand out of your mouth,
but play my game by keeping still.
I pat the mound until it's firm.
I decorate your grave with shells.

Oh father, this is not pretend:
your shrunken bones and yellow skin;
the *tincture of morphine* I spoon
between your lips to end your pain.

Sometimes I sense you in the air,
a lonely ghost come visiting,
no longer ill, but as a boy
who in a clear high treble sings:

Praise God, from whom all blessings flow;
Praise Him, all creatures here below;
Praise Him above, ye heavenly host;
Praise Father, Son, and Holy Ghost.

NOTES & ACKNOWLEDGEMENTS

'Infant Sorrow': Spelling and punctuation are as in the original manuscript of *The Songs of Innocence and Experience.*

'Grandma's Bed': 'geyser' was a 1950s word for a water-heater.

'Hedgehog Girl': 'Hans My Hedgehog', a fairytale collected by the Brothers Grimm, relates the life of a boy who is born a hedgehog from the waist up.

'The Surgeon's Widow': Inspired by Marina Abramović's video tower of hands washing parts of a skeleton.

'Ascension': 'pinkfoots' is the colloquial name for pink-footed geese.

'Bone-house': Bān-Hūs is the Anglo-Saxon kenning for the human body.

'My Bed': Anne Bradstreet (*c.*1612–72) sailed from England as a founding member of the Massachusetts Bay Colony. America's first celebrated poet, she wrote 'Some Verses Upon the Burning of our House, July 10th, 1666'.

'Finding My Father': The closing stanza is from The Doxology.

Acknowledgements and thanks are due to the editors of the following publications in which some of these poems, or earlier versions of them, first appeared:

Café Review (Scottish Issue), *Compass*, *Dark Horse*, *Guardian*, *Magma*, *Poetry London*, *Poetry Review*, *Poetry Scotland* and *Riptide*.

'Mermaid' was commissioned by the Poetry Society and Beverley Festival for *Machinery of Grace: a tribute to Michael Donaghy (1954– 2002)*. 'The God of Sugar' was commissioned by Alastair Cook as a film poem and published in *Yonder Awa: Poetry from the Empire Café*. 'Home is Here, Now' was commissioned by Carol Ann Duffy for *Answering Back* (Faber), and *'1974'* for *Jubilee Lines* (Faber). 'Head Wars' was published in the anthology *In Their Own Words (*Salt).

'The Blue Wave', 'Forgetfulness', 'The Larder', 'Pomegranate Juice', 'Second Childhood', 'Travelling', 'Bone-house', 'All Kinds of Horses', 'Clementines' and 'Old Woman in a Forsythia Bush' appeared in *Second Wind* (Saltire), a pamphlet commissioned by the Scottish Poetry Library and supported by the Baring Foundation as part of its 'Late Style' project.

'Snow Queen' was broadcast on *The Verb* (Radio 3) and 'Finding My Father' on *Poems for Today* (Radio 3).

This book has been so long in the making and there are so many people to thank for their help and encouragement that I may have missed a few. Please forgive me if you are not on this list: Elspeth Brown, Mario Relich, Andrew Foster, Helen Mort, Rebecca Goss, Anne Caldwell, Carola Luther, Judy Brown, Lindsey Holland, Tania Cheston, Amanda Mclean, Fiona Gibson, Pauline Lynch, Hilary Hiram, Anna Crowe, Jane Mackie, Patricia Ace, Paula Jennings, Stephanie Green, Diana Hendry, Douglas Dunn, Jake Polley, Daljit Nagra, Dilys Rose. Especial thanks to Jane, Jessica and Esther Feaver, Kate Hendry and Stephanie Norgate and to my editor Robin Robertson for sticking by me. Lastly, thanks to my husband Alasdair for inspiring the poem, 'These Roses You Gave Me' and for his cooking and patience.